D0464341

a gift for:

_____

from:

_____

"People
rarely succeed unless
they have fun
in what they are doing."

-Dale Carnegie

secrets
happy
people
know

Copyright © 2009 Hallmark Licensing,
a division of Hallmark Cards, Inc.
Kansas City, MO 64141
Visit us on the Web at www.Hallmark.com

Compiled and written by Young Lion, Inc., Tulsa, OK
Text copyright © 2009 by Young Lion, Inc.

Editorial Director: Todd Hafer
Art Director: Kevin Swanson
Design: Sarah Smitka, The Pink Pear Design Company
Production Artist: Dan Horton

ISBN: 978-1-59530-008-9
BOK 5538

Printed and bound in the United States of America

secrets
happy
people
know

What You Can Learn from Science, Stories, and Simple Common Sense

GIFT BOOKS
from Hallmark

introduction

"Any day I wake up is a good day."
—Duke Ellington

Happiness. It was important enough for the Founding Fathers to claim as an "inalienable right" in the Declaration of Independence. But of all the rights humans expect—or crave—it's perhaps the most elusive and hardest to define. You know if you can vote, speak freely, or bear arms, but how do you know if you're *happy*?

Maybe that question is so perplexing because the pursuit of happiness can defy logic. As you'll read in this book's pages, in a survey of the most satisfying occupations, high-dollar, high-prestige jobs like doctor and lawyer didn't make the top ten, while low-paying, often thankless vocations like clergyperson and teacher ranked number 1 and number 3, respectively.

On a similar note, the average American's buying power has tripled since 1956. And just think of the medical and technological advances that have emerged in the past half-century. And yet the number of people who say they are happy has remained virtually unchanged—at about 30 percent. (*Happiness Is . . .*, Simon & Schuster, 2007)

This book, in its own way, is a pursuit of that elusive thing called happiness. What it is, how to find it, and even how to truly appreciate it. As you peruse the real-life stories, scientific studies, and conventional wisdom, you'll be happy to learn that true happiness isn't about fame, fortune, or professional success. It might be as close as the DVD of *The Office* sitting on your entertainment center, the dog slumbering at your feet, or the old friend waiting somewhere for your phone call.

With hope for your happiness,

Andy Fraser and the gang at Young Lion, Inc.

3

humor inhabits
happy people

Need a reason to maintain, build, or even acquire a sense of humor? How about this: Adults who have a sense of humor outlive those who don't find the humor in life. The medical school at Norwegian University of Science and Technology studied 54,000 adult subjects for seven years. At the outset of the study, the subjects noted their ability to find humor in everyday life and expressed their views on a sense of humor's importance as a coping skill.

As the study progressed, researchers found that the greater the role humor played in one's life, the greater the chance of his or her survival. The people who scored in the top 25 percent for humor appreciation were more than 35 percent likely to be

HAVE YOU HAD YOUR VITAMIN "L" TODAY?

Nutritionist and author Pamela Smith takes laughter seriously. That's because she knows that 100 laughs a day provide a cardiovascular workout equal to about 10 minutes of rowing or biking. And there's more happy news: Laughter stimulates stress release in the same way exercise does. Laughter, Smith notes, also helps fight infection by sending into the bloodstream some hormones that reduce the immune-system-weakening power of stress. ❧ Further, in a study of hundreds of adults, the ability to laugh—at oneself and at circumstances—was found to be an important source of life satisfaction. In fact, people who enjoy silly humor are 33% more likely to feel happy than those who don't.

(*American Behavior Scientist*, 1996, 39:249)

alive at the end of the study than those in the bottom 25 percent. (Skeptics take note: The study took into account variables like subjects' general health, age, gender, and lifestyle.)

In a subgroup of 2,015 subjects who had a cancer diagnosis at the study's beginning, results indicated that patients who had a strong sense of humor had a 70-percent higher survival rate than those with a poor sense of humor.

Sven Svebak, who headed the study, noted that previous research has indicated that humor helps people deal with stress and maintain a healthy immune system during stressful times. "Humor works like a shock absorber in a car," he said. "You appreciate a good shock absorber when you go over bumps, and cancer is a big bump in life."

The Norwegian study is supported by other research. Everyone knows that a healthy vascular system is key to a long, healthy life, and a University of Maryland study showed that while stress decreases blood flow in the human body, experiencing humor increases blood flow by 22 percent.

William Breitbart, psychiatry chief at New York's Memorial Sloan-Kettering Cancer Center, offered yet another insight on why laughter is good medicine. He notes that someone who can see humor in the side effects of treatment like chemotherapy might be willing to endure the treatment longer, "and that could be a way that humor affects survival."

"Laughter is an instant vacation!"

-Milton Berle

2

happy people
accept themselves
just as they are

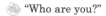 "Who are you?"

How would you respond? Some people define themselves by their job title, bank account balance, or the carefully maintained image they see in the mirror before going out in public.

But none of those things capture a person's true essence. And all of them can lead to a fundamental dissatisfaction with life–the continual striving for a more prestigious job title, a fatter bank account, or a more appealing reflection in the mirror.

Every New Year, millions of people make resolutions related to self-improvement. But what if the next time January 1 rolls around, you resolve, simply, to accept yourself as you are? To acknowledge that, yes, you have faults, but you are still a good person. A generous person. A good friend, spouse,

PETS ARE FAMILY, TOO

In the discussion about family and friends, pets deserve a prominent place. Animals have much to teach us about how to share and experience love. The closer we get to our pets, the more joy they give us. ❧ In their book *Companion Animals in Human Health* (Sage Publications, 1998), authors Barofsky and Rowan note that people who have a loved pet in the home are 22 percent more likely to feel satisfied than those who don't. Maybe it's time to call your local animal shelter ...

sibling, or friend. Someone who, every day, does way more good than harm.

Accepting yourself doesn't mean you become complacent or refuse to grow as a person. Instead, it means you appreciate your own value, and that value becomes the catalyst for self-improvement. Positive reinforcement rather than negative reinforcement.

Those who have studied self-esteem have found that people who accept themselves—those basically happy with who they are—can take defeat and disappointment in stride, rather than letting it destroy them. They refuse to be defined by life's inevitable failures. They see them merely as obstacles to be climbed over. Conversely, unhappy people make a practice of taking each defeat and magnifying it to monstrous proportions. They identify with each failure. They believe the failure is a sign of more to come. Instead of saying "I fell short of my goal," they tell themselves, "I am a failure. I'll always be a failure." (*Journal of Personality and Social Psychology,* 1995, 68:712)

Think of the close friends or family members in your life. These people aren't perfect. They've made mistakes, probably even hurt you somewhere along the road. But you still accept them and value them. Shouldn't you do the same for yourself?

"Self-trust is the first secret of success."
—Ralph Waldo Emerson

"One of the **greatest moments** in anybody's developing experience is when he no longer tries to hide from himself but determines to get acquainted with himself as he really is."

-Norman Vincent Peale

3

happy people
understand "tv or not tv"

Imagine going to a restaurant and ordering almost everything on the menu. When the food arrives, you nibble at a few of the dishes, decide you don't want *any* of some others, and completely devour one or two. Then you waddle away from the restaurant, over-stuffed, frustrated, and poorer, in terms of money and time.

No sensible person would feed his or her stomach this way, but this is the way many of us feed our minds, via television. We watch TV, not necessarily because we are "hungry" for entertainment or information, but simply because it's there. TV-watching, in a general sense, becomes a hobby. (Ask yourself how many times you park yourself in front of the TV because

"Live with your **whole being** all the days of your life! Your reward will be **true happiness!**"

-Rebecca Thomas Shaw

it's something to do, rather than because a particular show is on.) And this leads to incessant channel-surfing (or channel-guide surfing) in a quest to *find* something that holds our interest. It's possible to spend more time trying to find something to watch than one spends actually watching a program or movie.

Psychologists have discerned that some people watch so much television that it even inhibits their ability to engage in a conversation. TV-watching is passive, they note, and it can lure people into a "sit back and be entertained" mode.

The next time you walk into a room with a TV, challenge yourself to avoid turning it on, unless it's time for a show you really want to see–or you want to watch something you have recorded digitally. Then, use the new-found hours you'll have to do something meaningful with family or friends, get some work done, exercise, or read a book. Actively participate in life; don't let passive TV-gazing gobble up too much of it.

You'll feel like someone has given you one of life's best gifts–hours of time. And you'll be a happier person. In his doctoral research at the University of Michigan, P. Wu found that excessive TV-viewing can triple one's lust for more material possessions while, at the same time, reducing personal contentment by five percent per every hour of TV watched in a day. Do the math, and you'll have a proven formula for increased happiness.

happy people
celebrate their heritage

At first glance, the concept of America as one big melting pot seems charming: People from diverse backgrounds and heritages dissolve into one homogeneous mixture. The problem with this image is that in the "melting" process, the individual ingredients lose their identity. Nina Gomez, a professor at the University of Colorado, favors another analogy. "America is like a stew," she explains. "Each ingredient adds flavor, color, and nutrition to the stew, but you can still see and appreciate each one—the carrots, the meat, the potatoes, the celery, the garnishes, and so on."

"To make a
difference
in the world,
you must first dare
to be different."

-American proverb

Truly content people celebrate their ethnicity, their religious traditions, their history, their place in the world. They don't allow themselves to get lost in today's complex society. They stand out amidst all of the sameness of modern life. They never lose sight of who they are, where they came from, and how they can enrich life in a unique way. As a result, they feel better about themselves.

One organization dedicated to this principle is the Foundation for Empowerment, which teaches African-American children about their heritage via history and art lessons as well as activities connected to food and music. Students who participate in the Foundation's program improve their school attendance and raise their grades.

This principle has been demonstrated on a larger scale as well. In various studies of students, a strong sense of ethnic identity has been shown to increase life satisfaction by at least 10 percent. (*Social Indicators Research* 35:93, 1995.)

5

happy people
believe in themselves

"Believe in yourself" has become a cliché these days. And, like many clichés, it can be taken too far. Believing yourself to be a capable person is a good thing; believing you are incapable of ever making a mistake is elevating yourself so high that you're due for a long, painful fall.

The key is finding that balance between deifying yourself and dismissing the voices telling you that you're not talented enough, smart enough, or strong enough to succeed in life. If you don't have a sense of resolve, you won't be able to function effectively in life. This resolve keeps your chin up and your eyes looking forward, even in the face of those inevitable setbacks.

Speaking of setbacks, did you know . . .

Retailer R.H. Macy endured seven failures before his famous New York store finally caught on.

Baseball legend Babe Ruth struck out 1,330 times en route to his 714 home runs.

English novelist John Creasey received 753 rejection notices before he published the first of his 564 books.

Imagine the moments of doubt each of these individuals must have endured. But they never gave in to that doubt.

No matter what your goals in life, a solid, reasonable belief in your ability and a passion for what you are doing will make your efforts successful. And you'll enjoy your efforts much more as well.

In a recent interview, businessman (and former NBA star) Magic Johnson said that his attitude and mindset toward battling the HIV he was stricken with back in the 1980s have been just as important to his health and sense of well-being as the medications he has been taking.

No matter what your age, ethnicity, or profession, a strong belief in yourself will increase your life satisfaction by almost 30 percent—making you happier and more successful in both your personal and professional lives. (*Psychological Science,* 1995, vol. 6.)

> *"Don't wait to be motivated by someone else.*
> *Light your own fire."* —*A.R. Bernard*

6

happy people
know that age
is just a number

"Old age is always 15 years older than I am" goes the famous adage, and whatever "old" is to you, it's a place you're in no hurry to reach. People fear how age will affect them, mentally and physically. They can't imagine being as happy as they are now when they're "old."

Surprisingly, though, older people are just as happy as younger people. Many senior citizens report a serene sense of satisfaction with life. Further, what is possible at various ages is continually being redefined.

"Youth is, after all, just a moment, but it is the moment, the spark that you always carry in your heart."

-Raisa Gorbachev

Consider . . .

Swimmer Dara Torres was still winning Olympic medals at age 41 (while competing in her fifth Olympic Games). Actress Susan Sarandon didn't receive the first of her three Academy Awards until age 45. Mike Flynt (a grandfather) played college football—at linebacker—at 59. Walt Stack completed the grueling Iron Man Triathlon at age 73. Claude Monet was still painting masterpieces well into his 70s.

Today, advances in nutrition and medicine keep doors of opportunity open—wider and longer than ever before. Couple these advances with the experience and wisdom that come with age, and you have a formula for success and happiness that defies "old" stereotypes.

Stories like the ones above and a variety of studies and surveys point to one ageless fact: Age is simply unrelated to one's level of personal happiness. (*Activities, Adaptation, and Aging,* 1995, Volume 19.)

"The real trick is to stay alive as long as you live."
—Ann Landers

happy people
have faith

We've all seen the TV and movie stereotypes of religious people. The uptight, judgmental preacher. The self-denying nun. The frustrated teen who stays in her room, praying and reading the Bible, while all of her friends are out dating and partying.

Indeed, a life of self-denial and strict adherence to a set of rules doesn't seem like a life of joy. But a look at the facts— not the stereotypes—reveals a different answer. Life is complicated, confusing, and sometimes painful, and people of faith seem to have more tools to deal with these challenges. People from diverse religious backgrounds point to their faith as a foundation, as a source of answers and a source of hope when answers are hard to find.

And there is scientific evidence to back up their claims. Researchers at Harvard Medical School, the National Institutes of Health, and other organizations have consistently found

"Nothing splendid
has ever been achieved
except by those
who dared believe
that something inside them
was superior
to circumstance."

-Bruce Barton

that active religious practices bring people longer, healthier, and happier lives. Medical professionals don't know exactly why this is so, but they can't deny the cancer patients and heart-attack victims who remain upbeat and hopeful despite dim prognoses. James, a 76-year-old cancer victim, was told his chances of survival were next to nil. He was sent home so that he could benefit from hospice care for his remaining days.

James told his doctor that he didn't think his "time was up yet" and that members of his family and his church were praying for him. His doctor humored him but saw little medical basis for hope.

This doctor nearly dropped his clipboard when, seven years later, James walked into the doctor's office for a checkup. "Bet you never thought you'd see me again," James quipped. "At least not see me upright."

James is one of those living-proof examples of what the *Journal of Clinical Psychiatry* has concluded: Regardless of what religion people affiliate themselves with, those who possess strongly held spiritual beliefs are typically satisfied with life. Those with no spiritual beliefs, conversely, are typically unsatisfied with life. (*Journal of Clinical Psychiatry,* 1998, 54:49.)

"To know God as He really is–in His essential nature and
character–is to arrive at a citadel of peace
that circumstance may storm, but can never capture."
–Catherine Marshall

happy people
give themselves
something good to chew on

You are what you eat. Depending on who you are, that will come as good news or bad news. But few of us are perfect when it comes to eating healthfully. Have you ever felt hungry enough to eat just about *anything*, and the handiest option was a lethal combination of trans fats and high-fructose corn syrup? We've all done it. And inevitably when the order of fries or half dozen store bought cookies are consumed, remorse sets in. Who feels happy when his or her stomach aches and resembles a beach ball?

Like a car, we run better when our bodies get premium fuel. It doesn't require a degree in nutrition to realize that appropriate portions and smart food choices make us feel energized and satisfied. Lousy choices do the opposite. By filling ourselves with empty calories that ultimately leave us hungry, we encourage overeating, which causes us to avoid the scale, the mirror, and our favorite snug-fitting blue jeans.

Humans are complex beings with physical bodies that house our mind, emotions and spirits. We treat our *souls* well or badly by the way we fill our physical tummies. In other words, we consume according to the desires of our taste buds and the urgency of our growling stomachs, but we influence our minds and spirits in the process.

Fortunately, you don't need to be a nutrition expert or follow a complicated diet to immediately improve your eating habits. Anyone can take a few simple steps, which will make a major nutritional impact.

First, eat plenty of raw fruits and vegetables, whole grains, and "good fats" (such as almonds, avocados, cold-water fish, or dry-roasted peanuts). And note the word at the beginning of the previous sentence. Eat the good stuff *first*. Don't fall into the trap of grabbing a candy bar, then promising yourself you'll eat a carrot stick later—as penance. Healthful foods tend to be filling and satisfying, so if you give them first place, you won't be tempted by worthless calories later.

Second, beware of nutritionally bankrupt ingredients like high-fructose corn syrup, which packs loads of sugary calories without providing anything worthwhile in the process—no vitamins, minerals, fiber, or protein. Read labels. This stuff is everywhere, from peanut butter to ketchup to pizza sauce, to jams and jellies. But if you're willing to do a bit of nutritional detective work, you should be able to find foods and condiments that aren't dripping with syrups and sugars. For example, there are peanut butters with just two ingredients: peanuts and salt. But others are an unhealthy concoction of hydrogenated oils, sugars, artificial flavors, and—somewhere in there—a few actual peanuts.

Finally, ask yourself how you are going to feel *after* eating that preservative-laden sugar bomb of a cupcake wrapped in cellophane. Yes, that first sweet bite is a kick, but what about the aftermath? Did you know that just one saturated-fat-laden food binge can hamper your "good cholesterol's" ability to fight the build-up of the fatty plaques that lead to heart disease?

It's a fact: We are happier creatures with sharper minds and a stronger sense of well-being when we feast on excellent food. Next time you refuel, reach for a fresh piece of fruit or a handful of raw almonds or pumpkin seeds, and you're bound to feel content in body and soul. You'll have no guilt to weigh you down; instead, happiness is yours, knowing you've given your body what it truly needs.

AN EAT-RIGHT CHEAT SHEET

Looking for a few good foods to make your diet more healthful? Consider these.

1. Beans (and we don't mean refried beans): Good sources of fiber, magnesium, potassium, and folate. ❀ 2. Cranberries: These tasty berries help fight off urinary tract infections and may reduce gum disease and stomach infections. ❀ 3. Blueberries: They protect the urinary tract and aid the memory. ❀ 4. Tomatoes: They're loaded with the antioxidant lycopene.

For even more information on eating right, check out the following resources:

www.mypyramid.gov

www.health.gov/dietaryguidelines

www.nlm.nih.gov/medlineplus

www.myrecipes.com/recipes

9

happy people
know when
to call it a night

Did you know that 70 million Americans have sleep troubles—more than half of the adult population? Maybe you're one of them. Most people need at least 7.5 hours of sleep nightly, and coming up short hits us where we hurt: Our memories aren't as sharp. Our skin doesn't get the time it needs to repair and rejuvenate itself. Our bodies tend to store more fat. In fact, some health experts say not getting enough sleep dramatically increases our chances of becoming obese.

Sleep deprivation has also been linked to high blood pressure, diabetes, depression, and even heightened mortality rates.

None of the above is much cause for happiness, but the good news is that you can take all of the woes above and turn them upside down by improving your sleep habits.

Insomnia is typically categorized as short-term or chronic. Short-term causes are things like jet lag, the birth of a new baby, or a new residence, with its requisite new noises and sleep-interrupters. Chronic sleep disorders tend to be those that last a month or more, resulting from such causes as apnea (breathing problems), depression, or a neurological disorder like restless legs syndrome.

Treatment choices abound for those with all kinds of sleeping problems. There are non-habit-forming over-the-counter sleep aids as well as medical alternatives like biofeedback or prescription medication.

If a lack of sleep is affecting your health and robbing you of happiness, try some or all of the following suggestions. (And if you still find yourself fighting a losing battle with insomnia, don't hesitate to contact your doctor. Don't be embarrassed; insomnia can be a serious issue that fully warrants medical attention.)

SMART WAYS
TO SLEEP BETTER

1. If you wake in the middle of the night and can't get back to sleep, you might have sleep-maintenance insomnia. Try not to stress about the situation. Keep your bedroom lights low—or use a book light—and read a chapter of a book or a magazine article. Then try to go back to sleep.

2. Make your bedroom a Sleep-Only Zone. Don't make your bedroom double as your office and try to avoid watching TV in your bedroom—at least at night. The more stress you invite into your bedroom, the greater the chances one of these stressors will keep you awake at night.

3. Have a (virgin) nightcap. A caffeine-free drink, such as chamomile tea, can help you drift off to sleep. And, as tempting as it might seem, try to avoid alcohol in your bed-

time drink. Yes, it might knock you out, but alcohol tends to have a rebound effect, which will wake you up a few hours later.

4. *Go dark, go cool.* Keep your bedroom cool and dark. If your room is too hot, your sweaty bod will have you tossing and turning all night. And if your room isn't dark enough, your senses can be fooled into triggering your internal alarm with the message "It's morning! Time to get up!"

5. *Bathe your insomnia.* Not all sleep experts agree on the benefits of a soothing bath before bed, but for some people the warm water—and maybe some scented bath beads or aromatherapy candles—is the perfect prelude for a night of heavenly slumber.

For more tips, visit the web sites
www.sleepfoundation.org
and www.sleepassociation.org.

10

happy people
exercise their right
to be joyful

Do you remember being a kid—running through a field at top speed–just because you could? Just for the pure joy of going fast? What delight! To leap, climb, twirl in circles, run, bike at warp speed, and propel oneself through water are activities of pure happiness.

Challenging our muscles and cardiovascular system via exercise actually feels *good*. How sad that exercise has gotten a bad rap, and this simple truth has been forgotten–or distorted. Further, a good workout builds strength, agility, flexibility, and self-confidence. It controls your weight. It helps fight depression, and increases your resistance to disease.

EXERCISE DID-YOU-KNOWS

More than 60 percent of American adults do not exercise regularly. ❧ More than 72 million American adults are obese, and most of them would like to lose weight. ❧ According to research at Berlin's Free University, people with generalized exercise goals (e.g., "I will try to exercise whenever I get some free time") end up exercising far less than those who make a specific plan (e.g., "I will walk to the coffee shop and back every Monday, Wednesday, and Friday"). ❧ Self-control is like a psychological muscle, which needs to be exercised. The more you can overcome exercise-related excuses like "It's too cold to do my walk," the more will-power you build. ❧ If not used wisely, a personal trainer can actually lead to "exercise relapse." A trainer can help you create and stick to a fitness program, but once the sessions end, your resolve might dissolve. It's important to avoid becoming trainer-dependent by weaning oneself off of a personal trainer and striving to go to the gym and work out without his or her constant presence.

"The body wants to be healthy. This is the natural condition.... When the body is out of balance, it wants to get back to it."

-Andrew Weil

And you don't have to be a great athlete to enjoy the rush of the 100 percent natural stimulants called endorphins, which are released during aerobic exercise. Yes, being a couch potato can become a habit, but so can the positive, enriching and ennobling sense of well-being that a rousing game of tennis, a bike ride, or a simple brisk walk provides.

At 80, an age when many seniors are hooked on various medications, Ben is (healthily) hooked on exercise. If he finds himself getting a bit grumpy, he knows it's time to take a swim. Afterward, he exudes happiness, proclaiming how much better he feels—thanks to the two miles he swam. He says he feels like he leaves his stress in the depths of the swimming pool. And Ben's commitment to exercise doesn't benefit only himself. He inspires his children and even his grandchildren, who are shaping up to be life-long exercise enthusiasts just like the 80-year-old patriarch.

So be like Ben. Increase your energy levels, invigorate your body, and promote a positive attitude. To exercise is to exhilarate and to encourage feelings of immediate contentment and deep, lasting happiness.

Once again, let's run, spin, jump, bike, or at least walk for the pure joy that spreads from our well-toned limbs to our minds and souls that hunger to be refreshed. Let's exercise our right to be healthy . . . and happy.

"Remember,
man does not live
on bread alone.
Sometimes he needs
a little buttering up."

-John C. Maxwell

happy people
are encouragers

"When someone does something good," advised movie mogul Samuel Goldwyn, "applaud! You'll make two people feel good."

Encouragement might be the best gift for benefiting both the giver and the receiver. Life is challenging, and it's easy to get engulfed by our own struggles. But other people are struggling just like we are—and some of these people are close friends

"The happiest people
are those who do
the most for others."

-Booker T. Washington

and family members. It might be counterintuitive to heal others' wounds when we ourselves are hurting, but there is magic in stepping outside oneself to speak a helpful word, offer a pat on the back, or lend a helping hand to someone else.

That's because hope is contagious. You can't give it to someone else without catching a little of it yourself. Be sensitive to the pain others are feeling. Do what you can to ease it. Look for the good in others and be ready to celebrate it. Make building up others part of your daily routine.

Stir up some winds of kindness and encouragement. They'll fill your sails as well as those of others.

12

happy people
are friendly people

In the days before her death, a sickly woman was visited by a pastor. During their times together, the woman complained constantly about her family and various former friends and business associates who had offended her or betrayed her in various ways.

The minister tried to counsel the woman to avoid being so filled with bitterness, especially because her days on earth were numbered. But he doubted he was getting through to her.

A few days after one of their sessions together, the minister got the word that the woman had passed away. Just before her death, she requested that the minister officiate her funeral. It was to be one of the most memorable services of his long career.

As he took his place at the front of the church, he looked out at an empty sanctuary, save for the dead woman in her coffin.

"Find the good.
It's all around you.
Find it, showcase it,
and you'll start
believing in it."

-Jesse Owens

As he fought back tears, he truly understood the depths of this woman's bitterness and the shroud of loneliness it had dragged over her life.

If you needed incentive to maintain current relationships, rekindle an old friendship or patch up an intra-family rift, this should be it. Close relationships—even more than one's level of personal satisfaction or worldview—are the most meaningful ingredients in your overall happiness. In fact, being close to other people makes you four times more likely to feel good about yourself than if you don't feel close to anyone. (*"Experiencing Joy and Sorrow," International Forum for Logotherapy,* 1996, 19:45.)

Additional research sheds more light on this truth. The book *Mental Health in Black America* (Sage Publishing, 1996) studied core factors leading to a happy life. The primary components . . .

1. Number of friends

2. Closeness of these friends

3. Closeness of family

4. Relationships with co-workers and neighbors

Together, these four factors made up 70 percent of a person's overall happiness. So don't die alone. More important, don't live alone.

"A friend loves at all times."
–King Solomon

who wants to
be happy?
any volunteers?

To some people, the mere mention of the word "volunteer" makes them uncomfortable, if not exhausted. Given the overcrowded lives most of us live, who has the time—not to mention the energy—to volunteer?

The trouble with such rationales is that volunteering is the right thing to do. And there aren't enough people to do it. Most likely, your community is overflowing with needs. Libraries that need reading tutors. Thrift stores that need volunteer cashiers. Soup kitchens that need servers.

If the idea of stepping outside your comfort zone and your tightly packed schedule still leaves you cold, consider this: Volunteers feel great about themselves. They have a sense of purpose. They feel appreciated. And they are never bored. Ask any volunteer, and he or she will tell you that there is nothing quite like doing something good for a stranger in need.

The good you do doesn't need to be a lifetime commitment either. You can volunteer to coach soccer for a couple

"Do noble things,
not dream them
all day long."

-Charles Kingsley

months every spring or summer or serve meals to the needy each Thanksgiving and Christmas. The important thing is to try *something.* Leap over your objections just one time and see how it feels. A young man named Ray tried this. He agreed, reluctantly, to help deliver presents to needy families one Christmas. His reluctance stemmed from the fear that he would miss the two hours in the gym that he had been looking forward to.

When he and his band of volunteers arrived at an apartment complex, they found the sidewalks and stairs encased in ice. A quick canvass of various tenants produced only one plastic snow shovel—no match for the thick ice. However, the same tenant offered, "I do have this steel hammer . . ."

Armed with the hammer, Ray smashed ice for two hours, alternating right and left hands. When it was all over, he had completed a workout so grueling he could barely lift either arm. And the apartment's tenants could once again walk safely. "I learned something about volunteerism that day," Ray recalls. "It's a gift that has a way of giving back. Between the gratitude of all those people and the awesome workout I got, I almost felt guilty."

Ray learned something that day—something that research has borne out time and again: Volunteers, on the average, are fully twice as happy as non-volunteers. (*Psychological Reports,* 1996, 79:736.)

> *"Love stretches your heart and makes you big inside."*
> *—Margaret Walker*

14

happy people
surf the waves of change

"Changes aren't permanent," notes a hit song by the rock group Rush, "but change is." We all want life to progress on our terms, but it rarely does. Jobs are relocated. Jobs vanish. Marriages dissolve. Children and friends move away.

Some people are so devastated by such changes that they never recover.

Herb Score could have been one of those people. A promising Major League baseball pitcher, his career was hijacked

"The most difficult matter
is not so much
to change the world
as yourself."

-Nelson Mandela

one night when a line drive off an opposing player's bat struck him in the face. His broken bones and damaged nerves healed enough so that he could play again, but Score quickly realized that he no longer had the visual acuity, reaction time, and pitching mechanics needed to be an elite pitcher. And neither he, his family, nor his doctors could ignore the danger posed by further injury to his damaged eye. As a result, he knew he would never feel completely comfortable on the pitching mound again.

But instead of living the rest of his life in regret, Score took his knowledge and passion for baseball and put them into practice in the broadcast booth. For three decades, he was the voice of the Cleveland Indians, becoming as much a part of the team's lore as any player.

Like virtually every individual, Herb Score experienced significant change in his life. But such change doesn't affect everyone equally. Those who accept change as a part of life– and are open to the new possibilities it might bring–are 35 percent more likely to be satisfied with life than those who resist change. (M. Minetti, Master's thesis, University of Nevada, Las Vegas, 1997.)

> *"Blessed are the flexible,*
> *for they shall never be bent out of shape."*
> *–Modern beatitude*

money can't buy
happiness.
(really, it can't.)

Everyone knows that statistics can be misleading, but here's one that isn't: In the United States, the people who buy lottery tickets outnumber the people who vote. Americans, perhaps more than any other country's citizens, want to be rich. Or at least they think they do.

The truth is that people who are miserable when they're destitute tend to be miserable when they are rich—sometimes even more miserable. Those few lucky lottery winners quickly discover, for example, that their newfound fortune has brought with it family quarrels, tension in friendships, and a whole host of people and organizations, all with their hands out. (You might have read some of the stories of lottery winners whose spouses divorced them as soon as the check arrived, then demanded half of it.)

Further, you've probably read about the train wrecks that some celebrities choose to make of their lives. In a nationwide poll, the number one reason Americans gave for these celebrities' troubles was "too much money"–the answer cited by almost 80% of respondents.

Research indicates that this survey's respondents are onto something. In a collegiate study of life satisfaction, researchers analyzed 20 factors that could contribute to a person's happiness (relationships, career choices, health, etc.) The study concluded that 19 of those factors did, in fact, matter. The one that didn't? A person's financial status. (*College Student Journal,* 1995 29:438.)

Want even more evidence? Consider J. Paul Getty, the industrialist who founded Getty Oil Company. At the time of his death, he was worth more than $2 billion. However, he was married and divorced five times. He once said, "A lasting relationship with a woman is possible only if you are a business failure." Near the end of his life, though, he confessed, "I would have given all my money for one happy marriage." Now there's a revelation worth at least $2 billion!

"All material assets, in one way or another, will go away.
I really believe that happiness comes from the things
that cannot be taken away from you."
–Coach John Wooden

THE CANS AND CANNOTS OF MONEY

- Money can buy you a bed, but not sleep
- Books, but not brains
- Food, but not appetite
- Fitness equipment, but not fitness itself
- Surface beauty, but not inner beauty
- A house, but not a home
- Medicine, but not health
- Amusement, but not happiness
- Watches and clocks, but not time

"He is richest
who is content
with the least."

-Socrates

ON WEALTH
AND HAPPINESS...

Did you know?

* According to the BBC the world's happiest places are:
  Nigeria
  Mexico
  Venezuela
  El Salvador
  Puerto Rico

* Thirty-seven percent on the Forbes list of Wealthiest Americans are less happy than the average American. *(Social Indicators Research)*

* Americans' personal income has grown by more than 2.5-fold over the past 50 years, but Americans' level of happiness has remained the same. *(American Psychologist magazine)*

16

happy people
know
only YOU can validate you!

"Don't be so obsessed about other people's opinion of you! Why do you care so much what other people think?"

As kids, how many of us heard this parental advice, as we struggled to fit in with friends on the block or peers at school? Like a lot of parental advice, this guidance packs a lot of merit. The most well-adjusted people are those who

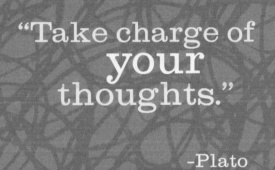

"Take charge of **your** thoughts."

-Plato

understand that their happiness does not depend on the opinions of others. They know that happiness is an inside job. They trust their knowledge, insights, and instincts. They allow themselves to evolve naturally, rather than be manipulated by others like pawns on a chessboard.

Whether it's which career path to follow or which person to marry, it's vital to trust yourself. That doesn't mean ignoring advice or guidance from the wise people in your life, but it does mean not being *controlled* by those outside voices. People have chosen the wrong major, the wrong career—and even married the right person at the *wrong* time—because they let extraneous voices drown out the one inside. And if something feels wrong, feels "too soon" or "too risky," it probably is.

If you tend to be a people-pleaser, try to stop looking outside yourself for validation and approval—in essence, letting *them* define your happiness. Take care of yourself on the inside, then let your inner light illuminate your life's path.

"Live with your whole being, all the days of your life!
Your reward will be true happiness!"
—Rebecca Thomas Shaw

17

happiness
is childlike

According to the Discovery Health Web site, children laugh an average of 300 times a day, while the average adult laughs only 17 times daily. What do kids know about happiness that adults are missing? We asked a collection of 3- to 16-year-olds for their insights. Read on and learn . . .

happiness is...

"The people who love me."
Kevin, age 9

"My mom!" Sergio, age 7

"My dog!"
Whitney, age 5

"Focusing on the good stuff, not the bad stuff."
Brittany, age 15

"Giving." Cyndi, age 10

"Caring about others."
Ashley, age 16

"Living joyfully with the people you love—
with no one judging anyone else." JJ, age 14

"A choice." James, age 15

"Having Saturday morning breakfast
at the coffee shop with my daddy." Liv, age 9

"My family." Patricia, age 12

"Happiness is boats and choo-choos."
Silas, age 3

"Being thankful." Dominic, age 11

"Being who God made you." Christian, age 12

"Appreciating what's around you." Hayley, age 14

"Forgetting the bad stuff." Josh, age 14

"Making new friends." Taisha, age 9

"Cherishing good memories." Brandon, age 16

"My best friend." Chantel, age 14

"Liking what you have." Martina, age 13

"Hearing 'Good job, Travis!'" Travis, age 12

"Hearing 'I love you.'" Jessica, age 11

"Happiness is what my mom has when I clean the house for her." Jennifer, age 14

"Being kind to others." Charles, age 8

"Happiness doesn't have anything to do with money. It's about bringing some joy into the world." Lily, age 9

"Hugs!" Taylor, age 4

18

happy people
can handle success

Olympic skier Picabo Street has made an interesting comment in various interviews: "Having *won* an Olympic gold medal—a dream since age 11—was harder than *trying* to win it."

The insight seems odd at first but makes more sense upon deeper reflection. After all, mountains of books have been written about facing failure, but how many books offer guidance on the pitfalls of handling *success*?

There would be a ready market for such books. How many times have headlines proclaimed the woes of superstars in various fields—sports, entertainment, high finance—who have self-destructed after realizing life-long dreams? In the aftermath of their success, they feel lost, as if they've been on a bullet train traveling hundreds of miles an hour—only to come to an abrupt stop. Sure, they indulge in the requisite "victory tours" and photo ops, but soon they are haunted by frightening questions:

"What if this is the high point of my life—and nothing else in the decades that come will compare?"

"What's next? How do I top *this*?"

"Do the people hanging around me genuinely care about me—or do they all want something from me?"

"Do I need to re-create this experience to have any chance of being happy again?"

Now, you probably are not going to win an Olympic gold medal or become the next American Idol. But chances are you will enjoy achievement in life—maybe even a major achievement in your chosen field. And, like Picabo Street, you'll be faced with your own "What now?" questions. And the way you answer those questions will make a crucial difference in your life.

We've all seen the mistakes: The actor who stars in a blockbuster and is so eager to re-create the buzz that he hastily takes a role in a flop, damaging his credibility and drawing ridicule from the press and from his fans. Or the athlete who tries to keep playing, despite the ravages of age and injury, and ends up embarrassing himself—or causing permanent physical damage.

In Street's case, less than two weeks after winning a Super-G Gold medal in the 1998 Games, she hurried off to World Cup races in Switzerland. On a Friday the 13th in March, she crashed, breaking her left leg and blowing out her knee in the right one. The surgery and requisite recovery gobbled up almost two years of her life.

What drove Street to race again so quickly after her Olympic triumph? The belief that "the only way to top a gold medal was to win two." In retrospect, Street acknowledges that she should have taken more time to enjoy her achievement, then thoughtfully and carefully set her next goals.

The lesson here: Be open to having a "second act" in life. For some, that means leaving a high-speed business career for something different, like coaching a high school baseball team or becoming a parent. Former President Jimmy Carter

IT'S OK TO CHANGE CAREERS

Consider the career paths of the following people . . .

- Gerald R. Ford — model turned U.S. President

- Dean Martin — steel worker turned entertainer

- Golda Meir — school teacher turned prime minister

- Howard Cosell — attorney turned broadcaster

- Tim Green — NFL lineman turned novelist and attorney

- Babe Ruth — bartender turned baseball player

- Boris Karloff — realtor turned horror-flick actor

- Clark Gable — lumberjack turned actor

- Paul Gauguin — stockbroker turned artist

- Steve Martin — magician turned comedian

- Albert Einstein — patent-office clerk turned physicist

- David Letterman — TV weather forecaster turned comedian/talk-show host

"People
rarely succeed unless
they have fun
in what they are doing."

-Dale Carnegie

is a prime example of this principle. After leaving the White House, he founded the Carter Center, a nonprofit organization that advances human rights. He also became a key figure in the Habitat for Humanity project, which provides homes for needy people.

And, as if that were not enough, he has also written best-selling books, both fiction and non-fiction.

Success in one discipline doesn't need to limit or define you any more than failure does. The truly happy person isn't addicted to success in one chosen field. He or she enjoys it, appreciates it, but then, when it's time, moves on to new quests for success.

"A lot of life is Plan B." –Anne Lamott

19

happiness
is traveling light

What's on your life's Wish List right now? What do you wish you had but don't possess? For many, money and material possessions top the list. Americans have a possession obsession: We want bigger, better TVs, faster computers, and MP3s with more memory and longer battery life.

For others, status, image, and success are the ultimate prizes. Some want to be the next pop star, game-show champion, or proud owner of a new face and better body.

Seeking "the good life" isn't inherently bad—as long as this quest is secondary to "the truly meaningful life." Unfortunately, the drive for material possessions and physical attractiveness can become all-consuming goals—a shallow, self-gratifying obsession with no lasting significance.

Truly content people have learned to travel light. They see life as a journey and determine to take with them only the bare essentials. They don't want the burden of unnecessary baggage. They don't get distracted by the glitter of money or the aura of fame and power.

They ignore the extraneous shiny stuff because they have an inner light—a light so brilliant that it makes everything else dull in comparison. This light, one of love and purpose, helps them find and navigate the path of true happiness and fulfillment.

So, what light will guide you?

"To take heart in the simple pleasures of each day . . . a patch of sunshine, a baby's laugh, or the comfort of being truly understood is to discover true happiness in life."
—Linda Elrod

"You don't have
to have everything
to be happy -
in fact, it helps
if you don't."

-Russ Ediger

happy people
live on purpose

What is your passion in life? What do you enjoy more than anything else in the world—the kind of thing you know you will never grow tired of? Maybe it's music, art, teaching others, or some type of creative writing. If you have found your passion, you know there is a sense of wonder about it.

Former professional baseball pitcher Dave Dravecky loved his sport so much that he confessed, "I would have played for nothin'." And today, he brings that same kind of passion to his callings as a writer and head of a ministry for cancer victims and amputees. (He is both.)

What about you? Are you pursuing your passion? Sure, there are required duties at home, on the job, or at school. But what about the world beyond the must-dos? Are you participating in the activities and pursuits you truly love—or just the ones

"To love
what you do
and feel
that it matters-
how could anything
be more fun than that?"

-Katharine Graham

you think will make you more popular, more wealthy, or look best on a resumé? What are you doing to ignite your sense of wonder and challenge yourself? In other words, are you making the grade—or making a difference? Are you following the crowd—or following the call of your heart?

An intriguing study of college students compared those who truly enjoyed their academic experience—and lives in general—with those who were uncomfortable and unhappy with their place in life. The major difference between the two groups was that the former—by almost a 2-to-1 margin—felt a sense of underlying purpose about their lives—an advantage that was missing from their less-happy peers. (*Social Indicators Research*, 1996, 39:59.)

If much of your life is sheer drudgery, you might be missing your life's ultimate purpose. Think about it: If you took away the paycheck, would you still want to do the job you have now? Would you "play for nothin'"?

You deserve no less than the best for your life. You deserve to experience a vibrant life in perfect harmony with the abilities and passions you possess. So don't let your life be a series of random events. Live it on purpose; live it with passion. You'll be happy you did.

True happiness is knowing that you are constantly in the process of becoming what you were meant to be.

21

happy people
put disappointment
in its place

What do you do with the inevitable disappointments that life hands you? Many people internalize them, let them creep into their hearts, where they fester and cause worry, pain, and despair.

Others are wiser, sharing disappointments with friends and relatives—or a psychologist, pastor, or counselor. People like these can be great sounding boards—and great resources for solutions to problems.

Do you make a habit of taking your disappointments to someone—or several "someones" who care about you? Let this be your first defense, not your last resort. Maybe you hesitate

"Happiness
is a light
that spreads from
heart to heart."

-Keely Chace

to share your disappointments with others. You might think, "I feel guilty complaining about my stupid problems in the face of all the important other stuff that _____ is dealing with."

If you feel this way, give someone a chance. Your friend might just surprise you with how much he or she cares about even the little things. Your siblings might astonish you with their helpful insights. That counselor your coworker has been recommending might be even better than advertised.

Think about the really good parents you know. Don't they care about their children's minor bumps and bruises and small problems as well as the major injuries and serious life difficulties? Would they want their kids to hide their small struggles and keep them to themselves? Of course not.

In a similar vein, does a good family doctor want to be aware of his or her patients' minor health problems—as well as the biggies? In fact, catching health challenges when they are small can prevent them from growing into something more serious.

Every burden is lighter when you have someone to help you share it. This is one reason that numerous studies—with young adults *and* senior citizens—have shown that close family and friend relationships are a crucial component in life satisfaction.

"Life is to be fortified by many friendships; to love and to be loved is the greatest happiness of existence."
—Sydney Smith

happy people
don't battle their critics;
they humor 'em!

The famous British leader Winston Churchill had just finished a rousing speech. Upon his final words, the crowd who had gathered to hear him erupted with a thunderous ovation. However, when the clapping and cheering ceased, one man, unimpressed by Sir Winston's rhetoric, blew him "the raspberry."

The rest of the audience froze in suspense, awaiting the powerful statesman's response to the rude critic. Would he scream at the man and publicly humiliate him? Would he have him thrown out of the audience? Churchill looked at his

"If you can't smile,
grin.
If you can't grin,
keep out of the way
till you can."

-Winston Churchill

tormentor and then spoke. "I know," he said good-naturedly. "I agree with *you*. But what are we among so many?" Churchill's humble and humorous reply was a hit with the throng, and the tense situation was quickly diffused.

Like Sir Winston, you might occasionally face insults or criticism from a jealous or mean-spirited nemesis. In such cases, it's tempting to become angry and lose your composure. And in today's power-is-everything world, conventional wisdom tells people to be defiant in the face of criticism, to fight fire with fire. Unfortunately, this approach usually leads to someone getting burned.

Don't forget the power of humility and humor to relax a tense situation. As King Solomon pointed out centuries ago, "A soft answer turns away wrath."

Certainly, there will be times when you must forcefully defend yourself or a friend. Be watchful, however, for those times when a clever, self-deprecating comeback can disarm even the most hostile of foes, the harshest of critics.

Remember: If you have your basic health, the love of friends and family, and some food and shelter, you are rich—rich enough to be able to afford some jokes at your own expense.

"Time spent getting even would be better spent getting ahead."
—Coach John Wooden

happy people
understand the contents
of true contentment

On a cool spring afternoon, an expert wood carver sat on his front porch, sipping lemonade and enjoying the view. Around him on the porch sat his various creations. A friend of the carver's stopped by for a quick visit and was surprised to see the artisan relaxing. "It's only 1:30 in the afternoon," the friend observed, "a little early in the day for a break, isn't it?"

The artisan swallowed a mouthful of lemonade and yawned. "This isn't a break," he answered, "I'm done for the day."

The friend, a young marketing executive, was puzzled: "What do you mean? It's too early in the day for you to stop carving. You need to produce more. If you carve more figures, you can make more money. You could even hire an assistant to help you with the business end of things. You could buy new tools. You could buy a shop so you wouldn't have to carve here at your house."

"Why would I want to do all of that?" the carver asked.

"So you can make more money! Are you dense?" his friend sputtered.

"And what would I do with all that extra money?"

"Why—enjoy life, of course!"

The carver sipped his lemonade again, then leaned back in his chair and closed his eyes. Before he drifted off into an afternoon nap, he mumbled contentedly, "Enjoy life? What do you think I'm doing right now?"

The lesson here? Life provides an abundance of blessings every day. And many of them are very close at hand. Make sure you don't get too busy to enjoy them.

"Where our work is, there let our joy be."
—Tertullian

24

happy people
savor life's flavors

Magic moments. You've had them. Chugging a bubbling soda after a hot day of outdoor work. Standing and cheering at the end of an inspiring song at a concert. Holding a little child's hand on a walk to the park or ice cream shop. Seeing that familiar smile burst across your best friend's face when you unexpectedly bump into each other at the mall. Having a relative mention *your* name when thanking God for life's blessings during a premeal prayer.

"A happy life
is simply the sum
of many small
happy moments."

-Penny Krugman

Every good and perfect moment like this is a gift. Every one–even the ones that seem like happenstance or coincidence. Life has a way of sending these gifts to remind us there is more good in the world than bad. Life offers a supply of love and kindness that will never run dry. And because of this, life is always worth living.

These gifts also remind us to keep our eyes, minds, and hearts open for the blessings, large and small, that await us in the future. Instead of dreading all that might go wrong tomorrow, next month, or next year, happy people spend their energy being watchful for those magic moments, the ones that fill our mouths with laughter and make us want to shout with joy.

So the next time life drops one of these blessings on your tongue, take time to savor it, enjoy it. A seemingly momentary blessing can leave a sweet aftertaste that can last forever–so let it.

Life will load your world with gifts, large and small. Take the time to open them all!

"Happiness is not a state to arrive at, but a manner of traveling."
–Margaret Lee Runbeck

25

happy people
set the right kind of goals

Thomas and Steve graduated the same year from the same college. Throughout their undergraduate experience, they compared report cards, girlfriends, job prospects, and even fantasy football successes and failures.

Steve usually came out on top in the various competitions, but Thomas resolved that he would beat his nemesis when school was over and "real life" began. After college, Steve landed a high-paying job at a high-tech firm. Thomas, a journalism major, earned job offers from a few small newspapers but turned them down because he didn't like the salaries—about half what Steve was making.

A few months later, Thomas signed on with an advertising agency. The money was good, but the hours were long and the stress levels in the office were perpetually at the boiling point. Most evenings, Thomas returned to his apartment, exhausted and frustrated. Some nights, he didn't come home at all, falling asleep at his workspace after a 16-hour workday. "At least," he told himself, "I'm keeping up with Steve."

About a year later, Steve called Thomas. "I guess you win, dude," he muttered. "I just got down-sized."

Thomas offered his sympathies, then hung up the phone. He thought he would feel victorious, but what he really felt was empty. He took no joy in climbing past his rival on the career ladder. His life wasn't made the slightest bit better because of Steve's misfortune. He realized that, for years, he had been competing in a game he didn't really want to win. He was making lots of money in a job he hated, in a business he had no passion for.

The next day, Steve began a search for a newspaper job, the kind he had really wanted for a long time. He ended up taking a 40-percent pay cut, but in the exchange, he found a job that he looked forward to each day.

Pursuing the right kind of goals is absolutely critical to a person's life satisfaction. If your life goals match your self-concept and your values, it will increase by a whopping 43 percent the likelihood that your career pursuits will enhance your level of satisfaction with life. (*Striving and Feeling*, Emmons and Kaiser, 1996.)

"If one does not know
to which port
he is sailing,
no wind is favorable."

-Seneca

happy people
pick their battles

Jason and his boss, Tammy, seemed to be in a constant state of conflict. They found themselves arguing about almost everything, from Jason's job performance to the department's mission statement to their differing communication styles. No matter what the subject, their unfortunate chemistry almost always resulted in an explosion.

Avoiding conflict and reprimands from "the boss" became Jason's constant quest. He dreaded every meeting, especially his weekly one-on-one staff meetings with Tammy. To avoid unpleasant confrontations, Jason tried to use e-mail for most of his communication, but, more often than not, the result was an endless back-and-forth of tersely worded accusations, insinuations, and justifications.

Jason felt like the mythological Sisyphus, who was doomed to spend his life pushing a boulder up a hill. But every time he got close to the top, he found himself unable to move the rock against the steep grade. He would lose his hold, and the boulder would roll back down to the bottom. He was imprisoned by a task that had no point and no solution.

After two years in a miserable work situation, Jason decided he didn't want to spend his career like a tragic mythological figure. He realized that Tammy held all the power on the job, and he wasn't going to "win" his struggle with her, no matter how much passion (or research) he brought to the battle. They simply clashed.

Jason visited his company's HR department and eventually secured a transfer to another division in the company, with a new manager. His job satisfaction skyrocketed almost immediately.

"I didn't fully realize how fighting a losing battle every day was destroying me," he said later. "And, to be fair, I'm sure it was no picnic for my former boss either."

Dwelling on unwinnable battles exhausts time and morale. Life is too short to devote energy toward something you cannot change. So don't keep fighting the same battle over and over. Try to arrive at a truce. Or, better yet, move on. Your brain, your stomach lining, and your friends and family will be glad you did.

> "Conflict is inevitable, but combat is optional."
> –Max Lucado

"It is in
the shelter
of each other
that people
truly live."

-Irish Proverb

happy people know
"together is better"

The emperor penguins of Antarctica know the importance of teamwork. They huddle together by the thousands, sharing warmth that allows them to survive the brutal, freezing weather—which can make a steel screwdriver as brittle as a pretzel stick.

The penguins take turns monitoring the outside of their giant huddle, on the lookout for danger or food. After one of the birds has finished its "perimeter duty," it moves to the inside of the group so it can get warm and sleep. The baby penguins stand on their moms' and dads' feet to protect themselves from the icy surface. If a penguin tried to survive alone, it wouldn't make it through one frozen winter night.

We can all learn from these penguins. Teamwork can equal survival. And the tougher the conditions, the more important it is for people to band together. You might not ever need to share physical warmth, unless your school or office heater goes out this winter, but you can share encouragement, joy, empathy, and ideas.

You can share the workload on a huge project or be part of a study group for finals testing. And there's something else you can share: the sense of success and accomplishment that result from committed, unselfish teamwork.

Wise King Solomon once noted that a "cord of three strands is not quickly broken." Imagine how strong a "cord" of 5, 10, or 50 of you and your friends and family can be. And imagine the fun you can have tackling life's tasks, challenges, and problems *together*.

"Talent wins games,
but **teamwork**
wins championships."

-Michael Jordan

jobs that serve up
happiness

Ever wonder which jobs bring the most happiness to those who toil at them 40-plus hours a week. A national survey conducted by the University of Chicago's National Opinion Research Center explored this question, and the answers might surprise you.

Firefighters, the clergy, and others with professional jobs that involve helping or serving people are more satisfied with their work and are happier in general than those in other professions, according to the survey.

"The most satisfying jobs are those involving caring for, teaching, and protecting others," said Tom Smith, the survey's director. Smith noted that jobs involving creative pursuits—such as writing, painting, and sculpting—also ranked high.

The survey was conducted with more than 27,000 randomly selected people representing a large cross-section of America. Interviewers asked questions about respondents' job satisfaction, general happiness, and how their level of contentment with the job affected their overall sense of happiness.

"Work occupies a large part of each worker's day, is one's main source of social standing, helps to define who a person is, and affects one's health both physically and mentally," Smith reported. "Because of work's central role in many people's lives, satisfaction with one's job is an important component in overall well-being."

Across all occupations, only 47 percent of those surveyed said they were satisfied with their jobs. Thirty-three percent reported being "very happy."

So, whose jobs make them most happy? Here are the Top 10 most gratifying jobs and the percentage of subjects who said they were very satisfied with their occupation:

Clergy: 87%
Firefighters: 80%
Physical therapists: 78%
Authors: 74%
Special-education teachers: 70%
Teachers (general): 69%
Education administrators: 68%
Painters and sculptors: 67%
Psychologists: 67%
Security and financial services salespersons: 65%
Operating engineers: 64%
Office supervisors: 61%

It's interesting to note that most of the jobs above don't command the big bucks. (Despite the impression you might have about "celebrity" authors and clergy, for example, most of them struggle to make ends meet.) Doctor and lawyer didn't make the list, due to the high level of responsibility and intense stress that come with both occupations.

And what about the least-satisfying jobs? Low-skill manual labor and front-line customer service jobs dominated the bottom of the list. As you have probably witnessed, some customers are impatient, demanding, and condescending toward salespeople, waiters and waitresses, and cashiers. So the next time you're at your favorite restaurant, think about what you might be able to do to make your server's day a little happier.

The Bottom 10 least satisfying jobs (ranked by percentage of those who report being "very satisfied" with their occupation):

Laborers, except construction: 21%

Apparel salespeople: 24%

Handpackers and packagers: 24%

Food preparers: 24%

Roofers: 25%

Cashiers: 25%

Furniture and home-furnishing salespeople: 25%

Bartenders: 26%

Freight, stock, & material handlers: 26%

Waiters/servers: 27%

100
things to be
happy
about

Low-fat ice cream

More TV channels = more choices

Satellite radio

Sunsets & Miles Davis

Running shoes look cooler than ever.

Southwest Airlines staff are a riot.

There's always a chance that boring meeting will get cancelled.

Video-store late fees are becoming extinct.

Johnny Cash compilations

Black-and-white movies on late-night TV

Computers keep getting cheaper, lighter, and faster.

The Simpsons ... still funny after all these years.

All of those flavored coffee creamers

Red wine is good for you.

More soda flavors than ever before

The healthful powers of pomegranate

Large-print books

You can create your own Web site.

High-definition TV

Dark chocolate is good for you.

Pixar movies

Spring is never that far away.

High school football games

Green tea—good and good for you

You can now record favorite TV shows and watch them whenever . . .

Turns out that eggs aren't really bad for you.

You don't live in the pre-automatic dishwasher era.

Used-book stores

That unpleasant task you're dreading? **You can probably delegate it.**

Friday is never that far away.

You look a lot better than that celebrity who just had another plastic surgery.

Firefighters ❀ Sunrises

Online bill pay

Burning your own CDs—or having a techie friend do it for you.

Garage sales

Fresh-squeezed lemonade

Uncomfortable shoes are out.

Some really good allergy medicines are now available over-the-counter.

Even McDonald's has some healthful stuff on the menu.

Overdraft protection

More pizza varieties than ever before

Most elevators don't play elevator music anymore.

Somebody has a crush on you, maybe even a few "somebodies."

Personal digital assistants

Bubble gum is still fun-and still cheap

There's a lot of cool exercise equipment for the home.

Our brave women and men in the military

Stevie Wonder

Baby-sitting is still a bargain.

Glasses are in—and there's a style that will look great on you.

High school musicals

Your signature looks cool; it would make a great autograph.

There's almost always a Seinfeld re-run on.

Hello, national Do Not Call list; goodbye, telemarketers.

Sports mascots ❧ James Taylor

Naps are in. (Call yours a "power nap" if it makes you feel better.)

The memory of your first kiss

It takes 26 muscles to smile; just think of the workout you'll get on your "happy days."

Fresh-squeezed orange juice

Automated car washes–part labor-saving convenience, part amusement park ride.

Someone you know and love made the Honor Roll.

Bubble-wrap is fun to pop

They didn't try to make a sequel to Casablanca.

There are more coffee flavors than ever—even for people who don't like coffee.

There's some loose cash lurking somewhere in your home; you'll find it eventually.

Disposable contact lenses

They've finally created some energy bars that don't taste like cardboard.

Books are still one of the best bargains going.

Milk Duds are low-fat.

Free samples

Regifting is still socially acceptable, if you're discreet.

You're still pretty good at ping pong.

The kids in your life like Dylan and Zeppelin as much as you do.

That thing you've been trying to re call? Don't worry; it'll come back to you.

iPods, all kinds of iPods

Saltwater taffy is delicious (and doesn't actually taste salty).

Sugar-free jams and preserves

Your favorite team will have a better season next year.

That pasteurized egg stuff means worry-free cake and cookie batter eating.

You still have some sick days left.

Church music now offers something for everyone.

Self-cleaning ovens

Check your calendar; there's a three-day weekend coming up.

Self-adhesive postage stamps

Blueberries: not just a delicious fruit, but an antioxidant too!

Free refills

You could be eating hot popcorn in about five minutes.

Johnny Carson Tonight Show episodes on DVD

Caller ID ❀ Room service

There are seven wonders of the world, not a mere five or six.

Babies seem to like you.

Peanuts comics are timeless, same with the TV specials.

Lots of remedies for the troublesome snoring problem (yours, or you-know-who's).

Non-greasy lotions

Postage-paid return envelopes

You don't have to pretend to like foreign films if you really don't.

bibliography

God's Little Devotional Book for the Workplace
2001 by Honor Books

Happiness Is . . .
by A.R. Bernard
© 2007 by Simon & Schuster

It's a Happy Thing
by Scott Degelman & associates
© 2006 by Hallmark Licensing

The 100 Simple Secrets of Happy People
by David Niven
© 2001 by HarperCollins

A Thousand Paths to Happiness
by David Baird
© 2000 by MQ Publications

1001 Things to Be Thankful For
by Young Lion, Inc.
© 2008 by Young Lion, Inc. and Hallmark Licensing

What I Know Now
edited by Ellyn Spragins
© 2007 by Broadway Books/Random House

If this book has made you
or someone you care about

happy,

we'd love to hear from you.

Please write:
Book Feedback
Hallmark Cards, Inc.
2501 McGee Street
Mail Drop 215
Kansas City, MO 64108

Or e-mail:
booknotes@hallmark.com

Look for Gift Books from Hallmark
wherever Hallmark cards and
other products are sold.